3 YA

HISPANIC BIOGRAPHIES

FRIDA KAHLO

Portrait of a Mexican Painter

Bárbara C. Cruz

Enslow Publishers, Inc.

40 Industrial Road   PO Box 38
Box 398   Aldershot
Berkeley Heights, NJ 07922 Hants GU12 6BP
USA   UK

http://www.enslow.com

ristina Elsa y Raquel Lauren, dos bellas mujeres de América Latina.

Library of Congress Cataloging-in-Publication Data

Cruz, Bárbara.
    Frida Kahlo : portrait of a Mexican painter / Bárbara C. Cruz.
      p. cm. — (Hispanic biographies)
    Includes bibliographical references and index.
    Summary: A biography of the Mexican woman painter discussing her work and its
international reputation, her political ties, and her relationship with the muralist
Diego Rivera.
    ISBN 0-89490-765-4
    1. Kahlo, Frida—Juvenile literature. 2. Painters—Mexico—Biography—Juvenile
literature. [1. Kahlo, Frida. 2. Artists. 3. Women—Biography.] I. Title. II. Series.
ND259.K33C78 1996
759.972—dc20
   [B]   96-851
                                            CIP
                                            AC

Printed in the United States of America

10 9 8 7 6 5 4 3

Illustration Credits: Archivo CENIDIAP-INBA, México, pp. 8, 12, 16, 28, 31,
40, 43, 48, 59, 72, 75; Collection of the Museo de Arte Moderno, Mexico City, p.
86; Collection of the Museum of Modern Art, New York. Gift of Allan Roos,
M.D. and B. Matheiu Roos, p. 14; Collection of the Museum of Modern Art, New
York. Gift of Mary Sklar, p. 65; Collection of the National Museum of Women in
the Arts. Gift of the Honorable Clare Booth Luce, p. 52; Peter A. Juley & Son
Collection, National Museum of American Art, © Smithsonian Institution, p. 38;
Courtesy of the New York Public Library, p. 67; Bárbara C. Cruz, 1995, pp. 20,
45, 54, 78; Photograph by Jim Reed, 1995. © *The Tampa Tribune,* p. 92.

Cover Illustration: Photo by Nickolas Muray, 1938. Courtesy of the International
Museum of Photography at George Eastman House, Rochester, New York.

CONTENTS

Acknowledgments

No book can be written without the help and support of many people; this one is no exception. I would like to thank:

my young friends Jack Vine, Lindsay Kettner, and Ryan Astaphan for their reviews of this manuscript. Although there were probably many more exciting things to do that summer, they willingly gave of their time and energy and offered the invaluable insight impossible for an adult;

my friend and neighbor, Jean Vine, who had a knack for providing moral support and encouragement when it was needed most;

my friend and Curator of Education at the Orange County Historical Museum, Michelle M. Alexander, for her detailed review and constructive suggestions;

my guardian angel, Mark B. Rosenberg, who facilitated my visit to Mexico;

and finally, my best friend and husband, Kevin A. Yelvington, who accompanied me to Mexico to complete my research and whose constant support and feedback were invaluable in the realization of this project.

THE LITTLE
BALLERINA

Frida and Alejandro felt lucky that they were able to catch the new, brightly painted, wooden bus back home.[1] They had just gotten on board when they realized Frida had lost the little toy umbrella Alejandro had bought for her. They left the bus and retraced their steps, but were not able to find the umbrella. Now, with a colorful cup-and-ball toy in hand, they found seats together in the back of the bus and hoped they would be home soon.[2]

The bus driver must have been in a hurry, too. He tried to quickly steer the bus to pass in front of a turning streetcar, but he misjudged the timing. The heavy streetcar could not stop and crashed into the bus, splitting it apart and throwing the passengers onto the street.

Alejandro awakened to find himself underneath the streetcar and the front of his coat gone. But where was Frida? After searching among the bodies for a few moments, Alejandro found Frida covered in blood with a steel handrail piercing her stomach. Another passenger's packet of gold powder had opened during the accident and spilled on Frida. People were yelling to help *la bailarina* (the little ballerina). With the gold sprinkled on her body, everyone thought she was a dancer.[3]

A man shouted, "We have to take out the rod!" He put his knee on Frida's body and pulled the handrail. Frida screamed with pain. She was carried to a nearby table until the Red Cross arrived. Her spine, pelvis, collarbone, ribs, and right leg and foot were broken in the accident. Her condition was so serious that when the medics arrived they did not think she could be saved and hurried to help others who had a better chance of surviving. Only five other passengers survived the crash.

After she was taken to the hospital, several surgeries were done to set the broken bones. Doctors were not sure she would live, telling her: "By rights you should be dead."[4] After they knew she would survive, doctors still did not know whether Frida would ever be able to walk again. Frida was only eighteen years old.

When her family found out about the accident, they were horrified. They were so scared of seeing Frida in her condition, they did not visit her. Only her sister Matilde went to the hospital to sit with Frida. Her mother was so shocked by the accident that she did not speak for a month.[5]

For a long time Frida had to lay flat on her back in a plaster cast. She was not even able to sit up. She wrote to her friend:

> Last Friday a cast was put on and since then it has been real torture. . . . There is a dreadful pain in my lungs and all over my back. I cannot touch my leg, I cannot walk, and I sleep badly. Imagine, for two and a half hours, they had me hanging by my head only and after that resting on the tips of my toes for over one hour, while the cast was dried with heated air. . . . For three or four months I must bear this torture, and if I don't get relief I would sincerely like to die.[6]

Although her healing was slow, doctors were still amazed at her progress. It seemed incredible, but within a few months she started walking again.

The summer after the accident, though, Frida had a relapse. Once again, she had to lay in bed, flat on her back in a brace. As she started to get well, Frida became very bored at having to lay in bed day after day. Her father was an artist and she had watched him paint before, and even though she had never

Frida months after the streetcar accident. She has carefully crossed her legs to cover the slightly smaller right one.

taken art lessons, Frida began to think about painting. Frida's mother had a special easel made for her so she could paint in bed, and her father lent her his box of oil paints and some brushes.

Because she could not leave her room, her first paintings were of her family and the people who came to visit her. Using a mirror attached overhead to her bed's canopy, she painted her first self-portrait. This painting provided a hint of what was to come.

In many ways the streetcar accident changed Frida's life. She matured. She found physical and emotional strength she did not know she had. But most importantly, she discovered a love for painting that would change her life forever.

LA CASA AZUL

Magdalena Carmen Frieda Kahlo Calderón[1] was born on July 6, 1907, in Coyoacán, a suburb of Mexico City. Frida always said that she had been born in the Casa Azul, the "Blue House," where her family lived, even though her birth certificate shows the address of her grandmother, who lived down the street. She claimed this, perhaps, to show the strong connection she felt to the family home.

Casa Azul had been built by her parents in 1904 and was originally painted white. Later, Frida would paint it a deep blue, the color of most peasants' houses and a color which was thought to ward off evil spirits. Like many Mexican homes, Casa Azul's back is to the street, with all its rooms looking inward onto a garden patio. This was the house in which Frida grew up with her three sisters, Matilde, Adriana, and Cristina. Frida was the third child.

Frida's mother, Matilde Calderón y González, was a *mestiza*—that is, her father was a native of Mexico and her mother was Spanish. She was a devout Catholic and very religious. Matilde was an intelligent woman although she had not attended school. She handled most of the family's finances. Frida said, "She did not know how to read or write, she only knew how to count money."[2]

Her father, Guillermo Kahlo, was born in Germany, the son of Hungarian Jews.[3] He came to Mexico in 1891 at the age of nineteen. Unlike his wife, Guillermo was not religious. He was an amateur painter and a professional photographer. At the beginning of the twentieth century, he was one of Mexico's most famous photographers. During this time, he was hired by the Mexican government to photograph Mexico's beautiful buildings and monuments. He photographed churches, temples, old and new buildings, and archeological sites.

In the painting "My Grandparents, My Parents, and I (Family Tree)," Frida's relationship with her family is shown. A two-year-old Frida stands in the center of Casa Azul holding a ribbon that connects her

Matilde Calderón de Kahlo, 1926

to her parents and grandparents. Her mother and father are drawn in their wedding clothes. In front of Matilde's skirt is an unborn baby—perhaps Frida before she was born. Matilde's parents, of native Mexican and Spanish descent, are shown over the Mexican land. Guillermo's parents, who were from Europe, are shown over the ocean.

Although she loved both of her parents, Frida had a special relationship with her father. In fact, in her painting, "My Grandparents, My Parents, and I," Frida put herself directly in front of her father. Some say that Frida was Guillermo Kahlo's favorite daughter.[4] In fact, he once declared that "Frida is the most intelligent of my daughters."[5] Recognizing her natural intelligence and curiosity, he would take Frida on walks where she would collect insects and plants to examine later under his microscope. On Sundays, Guillermo would take Frida with him while he did his watercolors.

Frida's mother, Matilde, was strict with her daughters. Frida would call her *El Jefe* (the chief) behind her back. Matilde tried to teach them her religion, Catholicism, but Frida and her younger sister, Cristina, often resisted. When the rest of the family prayed before meals, Frida and Cristina would secretly look at each other and try not to laugh. Sometimes they would skip their catechism class at church and go to a nearby orchard to eat fruit and play.[6]

At the age of six, Frida was stricken with polio.

"My Grandparents, My Parents, and I (Family Tree)" (1936), oil and tempera on metal

Polio is an infectious disease that often causes paralysis, or the wasting away of muscles. During Frida's time, there was no vaccine to prevent polio, as there is now. She had to stay in bed for nine months. Her right leg became permanently thinner and shorter. Frida tried to hide it with three layers of socks and a higher heel on her right shoe. Other children noticed the smaller leg anyway and would shout: *"Frida, pata de palo!"* ("Frida, peg leg!")[7]

Despite the physical handicap, Frida loved sports. Her father also encouraged her to play sports to strengthen her leg. She played soccer, skated, wrestled, swam, boxed, and rode her bicycle. Dressed like a tomboy, Frida zoomed down the street on her bike. Sometimes one of the other children's mothers would cry out: *"¡Que niña tan fea!"* ("What an ugly girl!")[8]

Perhaps because of her bout with polio, Frida entered elementary school later than other children her age. She started claiming that she was younger than she was. Later, she adopted the year 1910 as her birth year. This was the year when the Mexican Revolution started, and Frida was very proud of being Mexican. Because she was really born in 1907, this took three years off Frida's age.

Besides the love of nature and art, Frida and her father also had illness in common. Guillermo Kahlo was epileptic and had seizures (violent attacks), often when they were least expected. Frida said that her childhood was "marvelous because, although my father was a sick man, he was an immense example to me of tenderness, of work and above all, of understanding for my problems."[9] Later, when Frida painted "Portrait of My Father," she wrote the following dedication at the bottom:

This picture was taken of Guillermo Kahlo in 1907, the year Frida was born.

I painted my father Wilhelm Kahlo of Hungarian-German origin, artist-photographer by profession, in character generous, intelligent and fine, valiant because he suffered for sixty years with epilepsy, but he never stopped working and he fought against Hitler. With adoration. His daughter Frida Kahlo.[10]

Often, Frida went with her father on photography jobs so she could take care of him when he had an attack. She knew just what to do. Frida first had him smell a strong medicine, then she would put her finger under his tongue, wipe away the foam his saliva would make, and finally sprinkle him with water. She also had to keep an eye on the camera so it would not be stolen. It would be a disaster if it were stolen because they did not have money to buy another one.[11]

Guillermo Kahlo was very proud of his daughter in many ways, but he was especially pleased when Frida earned a place in Mexico's best school at the time—the National Preparatory School. Little did Guillermo or Frida know that the students who would graduate from there would go on to make great changes in Mexico.

LA PREPA

From the time the National Preparatory School was founded in 1868, it had been an all-male academy. By 1922, when Frida was ready to enter high school, La Prepa, as it was called, opened its doors for females. It was considered Mexico's best school at the time. Taking classes at the high school was like taking college courses.

Frida applied and took the difficult entrance exam. She soon learned that she had scored very well and had qualified to attend the school. Frida was one of only thirty-five females in a class of about two thousand students. Girls were very protected and discouraged from going to school with boys. One father allowed his daughter to attend only if she promised not to talk to the boys.[1]

La Prepa is very close to Mexico's central plaza where the National Palace and other important government buildings are located. This area once was home to the great square and temples of the Aztecs. When Frida went there, there were many stores, restaurants, and street vendors all around La Prepa selling snacks like *churros* (long doughnuts) and *nieve* (snow cones).

On most days, Frida went to school in a white blouse with a big tie, a navy blue pleated skirt, and a straw hat decorated with bows. Occasionally, Frida was bold enough to wear dresses she had designed herself, or even a man's suit.[2] Years later, her friends remembered her school knapsack. In it, she carried books, drawings, butterflies, dried flowers, and notebooks in which to write and draw.[3]

Frida often drew sketches of herself and others in her school notebooks for fun. However, art was just a fun hobby for her and she chose a program of studies that would lead her to medical school. She planned to be a doctor when she grew up. This interest in the human body would later appear in many of her paintings.

While a student at La Prepa, she was a member of the student group, *Los Cachuchas*. Cachuchas was the

The Zócalo (central plaza) in Mexico City as it looks today. The building on the right is the National Palace; the building on the left is the Metropolitan Cathedral.

name of the red knit cap they wore. The group was made up of nine members—two females and seven males. Frida called the young men her *carnales* (blood brothers), and the girls were like her *'manas* (sisters).[4]

The Cachuchas were known for their interest in politics as well as their pranks. They talked about how they would change the Mexican government. These nine young men and women went on to become important leaders in Mexico. They were very bright and talked about all sorts of things—poetry, art, history, and literature. Their favorite meeting place was the library. The Cachuchas had races to see who could finish their books first. Each of them could read in at least one foreign language;[5] Frida herself was able to read in three (Spanish, English, and German).

The Cachuchas also developed a reputation for the tricks they played. One time, several of them rode a donkey through the halls of the school. Their most famous trick was played on Antonio Caso, a well-known professor. While he was teaching in a large lecture hall, the Cachuchas lit a six-inch firecracker that broke the window panes and dropped glass and stones onto the professor. Antonio Caso smoothed his hair and went right on lecturing as if nothing had happened. The Cachuchas were never caught.

Frida was so mischievous that the director, or principal, of La Prepa once expelled her. Frida went to the director's boss, the minister of Education, and asked that she be allowed back in. The minister saw Frida's high grades and innocent face and demanded that she be readmitted. The minister told the school director: "If you can't manage a little girl like that, you are not fit to be director of such an institution."[6]

These years were very exciting and important in Mexico's history. The Education minister, José Vasconcelos, encouraged new programs in literacy and art. He believed that Mexicans would gain a better appreciation of their rich history if they saw it drawn on public walls. Vasconcelos assigned large areas of public buildings to artists such as José Clemente Orozco, David Alfaro Siqueiros, and Diego Rivera. These three artists became known as *Los Tres* Grandes (The Three Greats) of the muralist movement. One of the buildings they painted was the National Preparatory School. This is where Frida and Diego Rivera first met.

Diego Rivera had already developed an international reputation as a painter of frescoes (the art of applying paint to fresh plaster, usually on large walls or ceilings). He was especially known for his loving portrayals of the Mexican people. The Mexican government asked him to paint a mural called "Creation" in La Prepa's auditorium. With his baggy clothes, wide hat, big body, and fantastic personality, the students would gather to watch Diego paint and hear him speak. Frida was one of those students.

Soon after Frida met Diego at La Prepa, she developed a crush on him and announced to friends that she was going to marry him one day and have his baby. Her friends were shocked, in large part because they saw Diego as unattractive, too old, and married.[7]

Perhaps to get his attention, Frida was constantly playing tricks on him. She often stole food from his lunch basket. Sometimes she hid behind a tall pillar in the auditorium and, out of his sight, teased him and his wife, Lupe Marín, about other women in Diego's life.[8] One time, she soaped the school steps, hoping to make him slip and fall.[9] As she hid behind a pillar to watch, she was disappointed at the slow, careful steps Diego took; he never fell. The next day, however, the trick worked on Professor Antonio Caso, who fell down the same stairs.[10]

Frida's father's photography business began having problems while Frida was attending La Prepa and he was forced to mortgage Casa Azul. In her last year of school, Frida started working part-time. Eventually, Frida had to leave La Prepa and enroll in a business school to learn how to type. By taking jobs in a pharmacy, lumber yard, and then an engraving studio, Frida was able to help her family financially.[11]

During this time, Frida fell in love with the handsome and charming leader of the Cachuchas, Alejandro Gómez Arias. It was with Alejandro that she caught the bus in 1925 that changed her life forever.

Alejandro has said that "We were very good friends all our lives; we were more than sweethearts but never had wedding plans or anything like that, because we were still very young."[12]

As Frida recovered from her streetcar accident, she was also trying to keep her relationship with Alejandro. He was busy with school and other interests. Then, in March of 1927, he was sent by his family on a trip to Europe. He did not return until November of that year.

During Alejandro's trip, he and Frida wrote many letters to each other. On September 9, 1927, she wrote: "On the seventeenth it will be two years since our tragedy. For sure I certainly will remember it terribly well, although it's stupid, isn't it? I haven't painted anything new (and won't), until you come back . . . "[13]

After he returned they continued their courtship, although it was strained. At one point, they broke off their relationship altogether. It was for Alejandro that Frida painted her first self-portrait. In it she wears a romantic wine-colored velvet dress with a gold collar and cuffs. Maybe the gift did touch Alejandro's heart, because soon after he received her self-portrait, they were reunited.[14]

Alejandro went on to study law and became a famous speaker. Although the *novios* (sweethearts) eventually broke up, they remained friends for the rest of their lives.

THE ELEPHANT
AND THE DOVE

To a friend, Kahlo once said, "I have suffered two serious accidents in my life, one in which a streetcar ran over me . . . The other accident is Diego."[1] The first time Kahlo and Diego Rivera "accidently" met was when Kahlo was still a student at La Prepa.

Three years after her accident, Kahlo again met the fat, older man with the bulging eyes that she used to tease at La Prepa. As her interest in painting grew, so did her respect for the funny-looking painter with the fantastic personality, Diego Rivera.

Kahlo and Rivera saw each other again in 1928 at the home of a friend, Tina Modotti. Modotti was involved in the Mexican Communist party and gave weekly parties to talk about politics, society, and art. During this time, Kahlo gave up the girlish clothes she wore at La Prepa and began wearing the red shirt of the Communist party. She also began to paint in earnest.

Rivera remembers one day when he was working on one of the highest frescoes in the Ministry of Education building:

> I heard a girl shouting up to me, "Diego, please come down from there! I have something important to discuss with you!" I turned my head and looked down from my scaffold. On the ground beneath me stood a girl of about eighteen. She had a fine nervous body, topped by a delicate face. Her hair was long; dark and thick eyebrows met above her nose. They seemed like the wings of a blackbird, their black arches framing two extraordinary brown eyes.[2]

In an interview with a Mexican journalist, Kahlo tells how she and Rivera renewed their friendship:

> I took four little pictures to Diego who was painting up on the scaffolds at the Ministry of Public Education. . . . Without hesitating a moment I said to him, "Diego, come down," and so, since he is so humble, so agreeable, he came down. "Look, I didn't come to flirt with you or anything, even though you are a

womanizer [a man who dates many women at the same time], I came to show you my painting. If it interests you, tell me so, if it doesn't interest you, tell me that too, so I can get to work on something else to help out my parents."

He told me, "Look, I'm very much interested in your painting, especially this self-portrait which is the most original. The other three seem to me to be influenced by what you've seen. Go on home, paint a picture, and next Sunday, I'll come to see it and tell you." So I did, and he said, "You have talent."[3]

Sure enough, Rivera called on Kahlo that Sunday, and began a relationship wherein he said that Kahlo became "the most important thing in my life."[4] He began to ask for her opinion of his own work. Because Kahlo was so honest, Rivera sometimes did not like her answer. But in a few minutes or the next day he would realize she was right. Through the years, Rivera came to rely on Kahlo's judgment more than on anyone else's.[5]

Kahlo's father did not like Rivera at first because he was a communist and because of his age and appearance. Rivera was much older than Kahlo. Guillermo Kahlo said that it was like an elephant marrying a dove because Rivera was so big compared to his daughter.[6] When they got married, Rivera weighed three hundred pounds and was over six feet

Frida Kahlo and Diego Rivera's official wedding portrait, 1929.

tall—Kahlo only weighed ninety-eight pounds and was five feet, three inches tall.

Guillermo Kahlo also knew that his daughter would probably need expensive medical treatments all her life, and that he would not be able to pay for them.[7] Rivera was known to be rich and had a reputation for being generous. Guillermo probably decided that at least Kahlo would be well taken care of. In fact, soon after they married, Rivera paid off the mortgage on Casa Azul and allowed Kahlo's parents to go on living there.[8]

On August 21, 1929, Kahlo and Rivera were married in Coyoacán's town hall. Kahlo did not want to wear a fancy wedding dress, in part because of her sympathy with the working class. She borrowed her maid's skirt, blouse, and *rebozo* (shawl) and married Rivera in a very simple ceremony.

Because her mother was against the wedding, only Kahlo's father went. Before the service, Guillermo Kahlo said to Rivera: "Now look, my daughter is a sick person and all her life she's going to be sick. She's intelligent but not pretty. Think it over awhile if you like, and if you still wish to marry her, marry her, I give you my permission."[9]

After the wedding service, there was a big party at a friend's house. *Mariachis* (a Mexican street band dressed in fancy clothes) played nonstop, there were colorful streamers, and a lot of delicious

Mexican food to eat.[10] Banners that announced "Long live Diego!," "Long live Frida!," and "Long live love!" hung from the beaks of papier-mâché doves.

During this time, Rivera believed that only the middle class and the very rich used silverware, so most of the wedding meal had to be eaten only with tortillas, the delicious flat bread enjoyed throughout Mexico. Only for the soup were the guests given common metal spoons sold in the market.[11]

The newlyweds started living in Rivera's house on Mexico City's Avenida Reforma. Rivera and Kahlo had only a few pieces of furniture—a narrow bed, a dining set, and a little yellow kitchen table given to them by Kahlo's mother.

The young bride did not know much about housekeeping or cooking. Rivera's ex-wife, Lupe Marín, befriended Kahlo and helped her buy kitchen items and taught her how to cook Rivera's favorite dishes. Later, Kahlo painted Marín's portrait to show her appreciation.

After Kahlo and Rivera married, Kahlo began to wear traditional Mexican dress,[12] usually a long skirt, with matching blouse and shawl, and colorful ribbons in her hair. Kahlo's clothes began to symbolize her connection to her culture and history. Rivera liked and encouraged her choice of dress. In fact, Rivera complained that "Mexican women dress too much like U.S. women."[13]

H ere Frida is dressed as a Tehuana, the style of the women
of Tehuantepec, known for their personal strength and beauty.
This picture was taken at Casa Azul in 1942.

Kahlo called Rivera *Sapo-Rana* (toad-frog) or *Carasapo* (frog-face). With his bulging eyes and belly, it is easy to see how he got the nickname. In fact, Rivera often signed his letters to Kahlo *"Tu principal Sapo-Rana"* ("Your #1 Toad-Frog"). Rivera called her his *Chiquita* (little one) and often treated her as if she were his child.

Even though Kahlo and Rivera seemed to be exact opposites, they had many things in common. They were both intelligent, funny, had a sense of drama about them, had a love for Mexico, and sympathized with those less fortunate than they. However, their greatest connection was the respect they had for each other's art. Kahlo admired the political statements Rivera made with his murals, and Rivera prized his wife's distinct artistic style.[14] Kahlo once told a friend:

> I hope nothing will ever happen to Diego, because the day that he dies I am going with him no matter what. They'll bury us both. I have already said "Don't count on me after Diego goes." I am not going to live without Diego, nor can I. For me he is my child, my son, my mother, my father, my lover, my husband, my everything.[15]

Rivera was so proud of his wife's art that he once wrote to his friend, art collector Sam Lewisohn: "I recommend her to you, not as a husband but as an enthusiastic admirer of her work, acid and tender, hard as steel and delicate and fine as a butterfly's wing, loveable as a beautiful smile, and profound and cruel as the bitterness of life."[16]

Despite their love for each other, Frida and Diego had a stormy marriage. Throughout their life together, Diego continued to see other women. In 1934, Frida found out that Diego and her younger sister, Cristina, were having a love affair.[17] Cristina was Frida's nearest and dearest family member. Frida felt betrayed by the two people closest to her.[18] In a deep depression, she moved into an apartment by herself. To get back at Diego, she cut her long, dark hair (which he loved) and stopped wearing the beautiful traditional Mexican clothes that he liked so much.

Although they were separated, Kahlo and Rivera continued to see each other. They lived apart for about one year until they realized that they loved and needed each other very much. In 1935, they began to live together again. Kahlo eventually forgave both her sister and Rivera. After this, Kahlo herself had a number of love affairs with other people. Some of her friends felt that she was getting back at Rivera.[19] Rivera continued to be unfaithful and had a number of girlfriends about whom Kahlo eventually found out. Kahlo and Rivera began drifting further and further apart, sometimes not seeing each other for days.

In 1939, when she returned from her trips to New York and Paris, she was faced with Rivera's plea for a divorce. After a while, she finally said yes. She was working on "The Two Fridas" in 1939 when she received the final divorce papers from Rivera. In this painting, one Frida is loved, one is not. The loved Frida is darker-skinned, dressed in traditional Mexican clothing, and holds a small photo of Rivera as a child. The unloved Frida is lighter and wears the European clothing that Rivera disliked. From the photo, an artery of blood winds through and around the two Fridas until it ends with a splatter on the unloved Frida's white skirt.

Of their divorce, Kahlo simply said: "We were not getting along well."[20] Their divorce became final on November 6, 1939. During the next two years, Kahlo painted more than during any other time of her life.

Kahlo's painting, "Frieda and Diego" (1931) tells a lot about the couple's relationship. She shows Rivera to be a true artist, since he is holding a palette and brushes in one hand. With his other hand, he very lightly holds Kahlo's hand. His body is turned slightly away from her, while she, the admiring wife, turns toward him. The ribbon over their heads, held by a bird, tells the date and reason for the painting (their marriage). Using a ribbon to give this information is a tradition in Mexican art.

In 1940, Kahlo was again very ill because of her spine, her decaying right leg and foot, and her generally bad health. Rivera was in San Francisco, California, painting a mural. When he heard how ill Kahlo was, Rivera suggested that she travel to San Francisco to see her longtime doctor, Leo Eloesser. With Eloesser's care and Rivera's affection, Kahlo began to feel much better.

Eloesser also pushed the couple to think about marriage again.[21] Kahlo and Rivera again realized that they loved and needed each other.[22] Rivera told their friend Emmy Lou Packard, "I'm going to marry her because she really needs me," and he really needed Frida, too.[23] On December 8, 1940—Rivera's fifty-fourth birthday—the two were married for the second time.

When they returned to Mexico, Kahlo decided that she needed to concentrate on her work and build a life for herself.[24] She and Rivera moved into Casa Azul in Coyoacán while Rivera continued to use his studio in San Angel.

The five years following their second wedding were the most peaceful of their marriage together. They enjoyed simply being together and sharing daily life.[25] In a letter to Rivera, Kahlo told him that she loved him "more than my own skin."[26] Later, Rivera said that "the most wonderful part of my life had been my love for Frida."[27]

EL NORTE

Kahlo had first left Mexico in the fall of 1930. Her husband, Diego Rivera, had been asked to paint two murals in San Francisco. While Rivera worked, Kahlo visited museums, spent time with the wives of Rivera's helpers, and painted several pictures of herself and friends. Even in the United States, Kahlo continued to wear her beautiful traditional Mexican clothing. When Kahlo walked though the streets, people would stop to look at the lovely woman in the colorful and elegant clothes.[1] One time in New York, when she was going to the bank, a group of children followed her calling out "Where is the circus?"[2]

One of Kahlo and Rivera's friends, the photographer Edward Weston, recorded in his diary:

> I photographed Diego again and his new wife, Frida—a little doll alongside Diego, but a doll in size only, for she is strong and quite beautiful. . . . Dressed in native costume even to huaraches [sandals], she causes much excitement in the streets of San Francisco. People stop in their tracks to look in wonder.[3]

Kahlo especially liked San Francisco's Chinatown. There, she bought silks from Asia to make her long skirts. To her childhood friend, Isabel Campos, she wrote "never in my life have I seen such beautiful children as the Chinese ones . . . I would love to steal one so that you could see for yourself . . . it did make sense to come here, because it opened my eyes and I have seen an enormous number of new and beautiful things."[4]

They spent six months in San Francisco. During this time, Kahlo was hospitalized for a short time for a problem with her foot. While there, she was treated by Dr. Leo Eloesser. Frida kept a lifelong relationship with the doctor. She trusted his medical advice above all others. Eloesser was well-known in California for his great skill and for the free care he gave the poor.[5] Kahlo painted "Portrait of Dr. Leo Eloesser" (1931) as a thank-you gift.

Kahlo and Rivera returned to Mexico for a short

Kahlo and Rivera in San Francisco, California

time in the summer of 1931. When they returned to the United States, they went to New York and lived for a while in Manhattan. Rivera had his work shown in a one-person exhibit at the Museum of Modern Art in New York.

While they were in New York, Kahlo enjoyed Manhattan by having lunch with friends, shopping (especially at dime stores), and going to the movies. Kahlo was very honest by saying that she did not enjoy seeing plays or listening to classical music nearly as much as going to the movies. She mainly liked horror films, Tarzan movies, and the humor of the Marx Brothers, Laurel and Hardy, and the Three Stooges. But what she really liked was to sit at a sidewalk cafe and watch people.

In the spring of 1932, Kahlo and Rivera moved to Michigan. Rivera had been invited to create a series of murals at the Detroit Institute of Arts. When they first arrived at their new apartment building, the Wardell, they found out that it was called "the best home address in Detroit." What Kahlo and Rivera soon found out was that the hotel did not allow Jews to live there. Partly because both Kahlo's and Rivera's fathers were Jewish, Rivera confronted the owner and shouted "We are going to have to leave!" They demanded that the rule against Jews be removed. The owner eventually agreed, and even lowered the rent from $185 to $100 a month.[6]

Kahlo and Rivera at Jones Beach, New York, 1933

The time in Detroit was a lonely time for Kahlo, since Rivera was very busy with his work. He worked fourteen to fifteen hours each day and many of these hours were in the middle of the night. Rivera often started painting at midnight, after his helpers had prepared a part of the wall that he was supposed to paint. Once he even fell from a tall scaffold and got hurt because he had fallen asleep while he worked.

Even though she had some pleasant memories of San Francisco, Kahlo often called the United States "Gringolandia," (land of the Gringos or whites) and did not seem to like it very much. She felt that many of the houses in Detroit were dirty and neglected and called the city "the shabby old village."[7] Kahlo especially disliked big apartment buildings, calling them chicken coops. She felt that American food was tasteless and missed her Mexican dishes. Kahlo finally found a few small grocery stores in Detroit that had Mexican food and was able to cook some Mexican meals. Still, she was not comfortable cooking on the modern electric stove, preferring the traditional kitchens of Mexico.[8] She even found Americans' pale faces unattractive, comparing them to "unbaked rolls."[9]

Her memories of the homeless in New York also left a bad impression on Kahlo. In a letter to Eloesser, she wrote:

> High society here turns me off and I feel a bit of rage against all these rich guys here, since I have seen thousands of people in the most terrible misery without anything to eat and with no place to sleep, that is what has most impressed me here, it is terrifying to see the rich having parties day and night while thousands and thousands of people are dying of hunger.[10]

While she was in Detroit, Kahlo found out she was pregnant. She was told by her doctor to stay quietly in bed, but by the summer, Kahlo began feeling very sick. On the night of July 4, 1932, Kahlo was rushed to Henry Ford Hospital. She lost a lot of blood and she lost the child. After she recuperated, she retold the story and her disappointment at not being able to have a baby by painting "Henry Ford Hospital" (1932). Doctors told Kahlo that because of her accident in 1925, it would be foolish to try to have any more children.

The year 1932 was also a very sad year for Kahlo because her mother died, after having developed breast cancer six months before.[11] Kahlo made a trip back to Mexico by train to attend her mother's funeral. After this experience, she painted "My Birth" (1932) in which she shows her mother Matilde giving birth to her. She stayed in Mexico for five weeks keeping her father company. During Kahlo's trip to Mexico she realized how much she missed her family and friends.

When Kahlo returned to Detroit, she begged Rivera to move back to Mexico with her. Rivera refused. He liked living in the United States and after the Detroit murals, Rivera had a job creating a mural at Rockefeller Center in New York.

During this time, Kahlo painted "My Dress Hangs There" (1933). In this painting, Kahlo shows her disappointment and disgust with North American culture. This is the only artwork where Kahlo combined oil painting and collàge (putting together different types of materials). In it, a traditional Mexican dress symbolizing Kahlo hangs between a toilet and a sports trophy. Every single object in the painting represents something that Kahlo found wrong with the United States.

Another source of unhappiness for Kahlo was the Rockefeller Center scandal. Rivera was almost finished with the mural when he was fired from the project. Nelson Rockefeller asked that he remove a picture of the communist leader Vladimir Lenin from the mural.

Frida Kahlo (right), Diego Rivera, and his assistant, Lucienne Bloch (left), at the New Worker's School in New York, 1933. After being fired by Nelson Rockefeller, Rivera painted several murals here.

Because Rockefeller was a wealthy businessperson, it upset him that a portrait of a communist (who criticized businesspeople like Rockefeller) would be included in the mural. Rivera refused to remove Lenin's picture.

Five days later, Rockefeller gave Diego a check for the rest of the money due him and told him to stop working at once. (Of the $21,000 fee, Rivera was left with only $7,000 after paying his assistants and his agent, and deducting the cost of the painting materials.[12])

The conflict was big news. The *New York World-Telegram* printed an article with the title "Rivera Paints Scenes of Communist Activity and John D. Jr. Foots Bill."[13] People thought it was strange that a millionaire businessperson like Rockefeller would pay an artist to paint anything associated with communism.

Many people were upset at Rivera's communist politics, but many others asked Rockefeller to rethink his decision. Crowds gathered outside with signs in support of the artist. Rockefeller would not change his position, and nine months later had the mural destroyed. Finally, in late 1933, after the Rockefeller Center scandal, Rivera agreed to return to Mexico. After almost four years of living in the United States, Kahlo was ready to go back home. Because they were short of funds, friends raised money for Kahlo and Rivera to get back to Mexico.

The twin houses in San Angel

When they arrived in Mexico, they moved into twin houses in San Angel that had been built especially for them. They lived in the smaller blue house, which also held Kahlo's studio. The larger pink house was Rivera's studio. On the roof, a bridge connected the two houses. Sometimes, when Kahlo was angry at Rivera, she would lock the door on her side of the bridge so he could not get inside. Through the closed door, Rivera would beg Kahlo to forgive him.[14] Kahlo and Rivera lived there until 1939 when they divorced and Kahlo moved back to Casa Azul. The twin houses still stand today in San Angel on the corner of Altavista and Diego Rivera Streets.

CHAPTER SIX

¡VIVA MÉXICO!

 Trying to solve the problems of society was very important to Kahlo. Since she was a young girl, Kahlo was regularly involved in politics.[1] As a member of the Young Communist League in Mexico, she agreed with the goal of the communists, to change the Mexican social system for the betterment of the working class.

While Kahlo was healing from her accident in 1925, many friends visited her. One of them was Germán de Campo, a young man who strongly believed in communist politics. Communism is a system in which property is owned in common. That means that all farms, factories, and other property are owned by the state to benefit all people. Sometimes communism is also called "Marxism" after Karl Marx, the German thinker who wrote on the subject.

Germán de Campo introduced Kahlo to Tina Modotti in 1928. Modotti was a beautiful Italian photographer who had moved to Mexico in 1923. Modotti held parties for artists, writers, and intellectuals. She was also involved in the production of the Mexican communist newspaper, *El Machete*. Modotti became famous in part because she was one of the first women to wear jeans in Mexico.[2] It was Modotti who encouraged Kahlo to join the Communist party.[3]

Modotti and Kahlo had many things in common. They both enjoyed art—Modotti was a photographer and Kahlo, a painter. They were both concerned about Mexico's poor—especially women and children. They were both strong, independent women. Many years later, at an exhibition of Kahlo's paintings and Modotti's photographs, one art critic called it "an impressive show of two powerful but compassionate women who lived adventurous lives."[4]

Kahlo not only admired Tina Modotti's beliefs in communism, but also how she lived her daily life based on those strong beliefs. Many of Modotti's photographs were of Mexico's peasants. Kahlo also wanted to show her commitment: she cut her hair very short and started wearing the red and black shirts of the Communist party. She also started wearing a pin that had the hammer and sickle, a symbol of the Soviet Union's Communist party.

Although Kahlo was a member of the Mexican Communist party, she missed many of the meetings. Her friend Concha Michel believes that Kahlo stopped going because women were still not treated as men's equals. At this time, women were mostly typists, messengers, and assistants.[5] Mexican women did not even have full voting rights until 1958.

It was at Modotti's house that Kahlo and Rivera had seen each other for the first time since Kahlo's

Kahlo and Rivera marching with the Syndicate of Technical Workers, Painters, and Sculptors

days as a student at La Prepa. One of the things that attracted them to each other was their interest and support of socialist politics. When Rivera included Kahlo in his mural "Distributing Arms" (1928), he painted her in a red shirt passing out weapons to peasants. This mural can still be seen at the Ministry of Education in Mexico City.

Rivera was asked by several Americans to create murals in the United States. But when Kahlo and Rivera first traveled to the United States in 1930, Rivera was almost not allowed in. Because of Rivera's Communist background, his entry visa was denied. At the time, people who were active in the Communist party were considered threats to the United States. With the help of Albert Bender, a powerful business-person, the United States government finally allowed Rivera to enter the country.[6] Bender had visited Mexico earlier, and after admiring Rivera's paintings, bought several of them. It is Albert Bender's name that appears on the ribbon in Kahlo's 1931 piece, "Frida and Diego Rivera."

Three years later, Rivera was asked to create the mural for the Rockefeller Center in New York. When Rockefeller and the artist clashed over Lenin's portrait, Kahlo sided with her husband and defended him publicly in several interviews. Kahlo and Rivera had the last laugh, though. In 1934, he repainted the same mural in the Palace of Fine Arts in Mexico City. He added a portrait of Rockefeller in which he is portrayed negatively.

Another communist controversy in which Kahlo and Rivera were involved was the exile of Leon Trotsky. Trotsky, along with Vladimir Lenin and Joseph Stalin, was instrumental in bringing about the Russian Revolution in 1917. Up to this time, Russia had been ruled by the czars (kings) of the House of Romanov for three hundred years. While the House of Romanov lived in luxury, most Russians were poor and had to work very hard for their meager existence. By 1917, the Russian people were tired of being hungry, jobless, and having no voice in government. Nicholas II, the czar of Russia, was dethroned and a communist government was put in place. The new leaders promised a new society where all Russians would have equal shares of the country's wealth.

Almost from the beginning, however, Trotsky, Lenin, and Stalin had serious disagreements about how to run the new government. After Lenin died in 1924, Joseph Stalin became the sole head of state. Soon, Leon Trotsky was ordered out of the Soviet Union by Stalin. For nine years, Trotsky and his wife, Natalia Sedova, lived in central Asia, Turkey, France, and Norway.

After a few years of moving from place to place, Trotsky had nowhere else to go. Rivera learned of Trotsky's situation and asked Mexican president

Lázaro Cárdenas to allow Trotsky into the country. Rivera was surprised but pleased when President Cárdenas said yes.[7]

In January 1937, Leon Trotsky (who was then seventy-four years old) and his wife moved into Kahlo's Casa Azul in Coyoacán, while Kahlo and Rivera lived in their twin houses in San Angel. Because there were people who did not like Trotsky, Casa Azul had to be supplied with guards, alarms, and covered windows. The couple lived there for two years.

During this time, Kahlo had a love affair with Leon Trotsky. Trotsky was captivated by Kahlo's exotic beauty and talent, while Kahlo was flattered by the intellectual's interest. When they feared that their spouses would find out, they broke it off and decided to stay friends.[8] In 1937, she painted a self-portrait that shows her holding a piece of paper that says, "To Trotsky with much affection, I dedicate this painting November 7, 1937." The date of November 7 was important because it was both Trotsky's birthday and the anniversary of the Russian Revolution.

The friendship between Rivera and Trotsky was not to last, however. They began having arguments over politics. They quarrelled about the Soviet Union, about Mexican politics, and about trade unions. Finally, in April 1939, Trotsky moved out of La Casa Azul to another house nearby.

"Self-Portrait Dedicated to Leon Trotsky" (1937)

The following year, Stalin, the leader of the Soviet Union, sent a spy named Ramón Mercader to kill Trotsky. Anyone who knew Mercader was suspected of helping him in the murder. Because Frida and her sister Cristina once had had dinner with Mercader, they were questioned by police for hours and held in jail. When after two days of questioning it became apparent that neither Frida nor Cristina were involved in the assassination, the two sisters were finally allowed to go home.

Kahlo continued her involvement in communist politics throughout her life. When she became a teacher, she had the opportunity to teach others about her beliefs. In 1943, Kahlo became a teacher of poor high school students who showed promise in art. The school was locally known as *La Esmeralda* (the emerald) because that was the name of the street it was on. During her time as a teacher there, Kahlo shared her political beliefs with her art students.

One of Kahlo's students, Guillermo Monroy, remembers the first day of class:

> She [Frida] appeared there all of a sudden like a stupendous flowering branch because of her joyfulness, kindness, and enchantment. . . . The young people who were going to be her students . . . received her with true enthusiasm and emotion. She chatted with us briefly after greeting us very affectionately, and then immediately told us in a very animated way:

Leon Trotsky's grave in Coyoacán, Mexico. Trotsky was killed on August 21, 1940.

"Well, kids, let's go to work; I will be your so-called teacher, [although] I am not any such thing, I only want to be your friend, I never have been a painting teacher, nor do I think I ever will be, since I am always learning . . . I hope you will not be bored with me, and when I seem a bore to you, I ask you, please, not to keep quiet, all right?"[9]

Monroy remembers that after this introduction, Kahlo asked her new students what they wanted to paint. The group was silent for a few moments, surprised at the question. Usually they were told what to paint. Finally, Monroy, seeing how pretty Kahlo was, asked her to pose for them. Kahlo was very touched by the request. She asked for a chair and with a slight smile she sat down and posed for the students.

Unfortunately, after a few months of working at La Esmeralda, Kahlo found that the long trip between her home in Coyoacán and the school was a strain on her health. Since she did not want to stop teaching, she asked the students to come to her home instead. At first many students came to Kahlo's house. After a while, because it was such a long bus ride, there were only four students left. These four students—three young men and one woman—came to be called "Los Fridos" and studied formally under Kahlo for three years, although they continued their relationship with her after their graduation.

Kahlo taught Los Fridos all about Mexican art, both old and new. In addition, she also recommended Marxist books and involved them in political discussions and demonstrations. She told them that painting should "play a role in society."[10] To illustrate this, Kahlo took them on field trips to where *Los Tres Grandes*, the Three Greats, (José Orozco, David Siqueiros, and Diego Rivera) were working.

After a time, Los Fridos created an organization of painters who believed in sharing their art with the common people. They called themselves the Young Revolutionary Artists and grew to forty-seven members. They brought their art to different working-class sections of Mexico City on market day, when they knew that many of the people gathered to do their shopping.

Kahlo got permission for Los Fridos to paint murals on the walls of La Rosita, a *pulquería*. A pulquería is a bar for peasants or working-class people that serves *pulque*, a strong drink. La Rosita was close to Kahlo's house, on the corner of Londres Street. Kahlo and Rivera supplied the paint and brushes and offered advice as the work progressed. Kahlo's art students produced several murals at La Rosita, but they were later destroyed when another building was constructed there.

Los Fridos also painted the walls of a public laundry. The government had built the laundry for the women who made their living by washing other people's clothes. Los Fridos painted murals that showed the women not only hard at work, but also enjoying a simple meal together. The laundry women were very thankful to the young artists for portraying them in such a proud way. When the murals were completed, a celebration was held with food and music. Even though she was in pain, her movement restricted by the braces on her body, Kahlo would go to the unveiling of her students' murals, proud of their hard work.

The four original students are still friends even to this day. They are proud to be called Los Fridos. Even though they are all artists, they each have their own special style. What they do have in common is their sympathy for Mexico's poor and their love of Mexican culture. When Los Fridos graduated from La Esmeralda, Kahlo was sad, but Rivera reminded her that "It is the moment in which they are going to walk alone. Even though they go their own ways, they will come and visit us always, because they are our comrades."[11] Indeed, even after they graduated, Los Fridos continued to visit their teacher for many years.

Kahlo worked very hard to change the Mexican government for the better. She cared greatly for Mexico's poor and working class. In fact, she once said that "I get on better with carpenters, shoemakers, etc. than with all that crowd of stupid, civilized chatterboxes called cultivated people."[12]

Many people remember Kahlo's kind words and gestures for those who were not as lucky as she. One of Kahlo's nurses and friends, Judith Ferreto, remembers that when they would go to the movies, Kahlo noticed the shoeshine and newspaper boys. Kahlo would say: "They always like to go to the movies. I know, because I was one of them, so please bring them with us."[13]

Throughout her life, Kahlo believed deeply in her communist views. She included some of these beliefs in her art. In the 1940s, Kahlo began featuring social content in her work. She inserted symbols such as flags and peace doves into her paintings. She included portraits of Joseph Stalin and Karl Marx along with her own. She even decorated one of her plaster braces with a hammer and sickle, the symbols of the Soviet Union.

In 1954, Kahlo painted a piece called "Marxism Will Give Health to the Sick." In this work, she painted a portrait of Karl Marx along with a self-portrait. Karl Marx lived during the nineteenth century and wrote about his dreams for correcting the problems of inequality in the world. In the painting, Kahlo is in a plaster brace and is being miraculously saved by Marx, who is portrayed as a saint. She told her friend Judith Ferreto that this was the first painting in which she did not cry.[14]

From left to right, standing: Frida wearing a man's suit, her grandmother, her sister Adriana, and Adriana's husband, Carlos Veraza. Seated: Frida's uncle, Frida's mother, Frida's cousin. On ground: Frida's nephew and her sister, Cristina.

Photographs of people Kahlo loved covered the headboard over her bed in Casa Azul. She had portraits of her sisters and father, her niece and nephew, and dear friends. There were also photos of socialists Karl Marx, Frederick Engels, Vladimir Lenin, Joseph Stalin, and Mao Tse-Tung, people she considered heroes.

Toward the end of her life, Frida's art changed. Because she spent most of her time in bed, much of her work painted during this time were of things that could be carried to the side of her bed, mostly fruit and flowers (these are called still lifes). In many of her still lifes, she included flags, political sayings, and other symbols. Sitting on an easel in her studio at Casa Azul is an unfinished portrait of Joseph Stalin, the Soviet leader. She once told a friend, "I only want three things in life: to live with Diego, to continue painting, and to belong to the Communist party."[15]

Some people do not remember Kahlo as being particularly political. In fact, one of Los Fridos, Fanny Rabel, feels that she was more of a "humanist,"[16] that is, she cared about human beings and improving society. One thing is certain: Kahlo was deeply concerned about how Mexico's poor, especially women and children, lived.

FRIDA'S
CELEBRATIONS

Although many people think that Kahlo's life was always filled with sadness and pain, many of Frida's friends "remember her as greatly enjoying life, happy, clever, and lively, always ready for fun."[1] She celebrated all sorts of holidays, birthdays, baptisms, and saints' days. In Mexico, there are many days associated with a Catholic saint. For example, January 17 is a day celebrating St. Anthony, who is known for his love of pets and animals. December 12 is the day of Mexico's patron saint, the Virgin of Guadalupe. On each of these days, special celebrations are held, and even though Kahlo was not religious, she used every chance she had to have a party.

Kahlo loved jokes, exaggerating stories, and funny words. She made fun of herself as well as other people. Kahlo gave people nicknames that made them laugh. She called Rivera's driver "General Confusion" because things would not go right when he was involved. She teased one of the workers in the house, Manuel, by calling him "Manuel the Restless" because he was so lazy.[2]

In addition to painting, Kahlo spent her days doing many different things. She wrote in her diary, including poems and watercolor drawings. Some afternoons she went to the movies. Other times, she went to Garibaldi Plaza where the *mariachi* bands would gather. The mariachi bands would be dressed in fancy costumes with huge *sombreros* (hats) and would sing Kahlo's favorite songs for a few *pesos* (coins).

Kahlo herself liked to sing, and many evenings were spent at La Casa Azul singing *corridos* (traditional Mexican songs) with friends. She and Rivera also had fun playing games like *cadavre exquis* (exquisite corpses). In this game, the first person draws a head and folds the paper down so that the next person cannot see it. The second person then draws the next section of the body and folds the paper down again. This continues until the entire body is drawn. When the paper is unfolded, the result is usually very funny. When Kahlo played, she used her wild imagination to create some hilarious monsters.[3]

Kahlo decorated Casa Azul with many items from the time before the Europeans arrived in Mexico. She and Rivera also collected folk art from many different regions of Mexico. The kitchen was decorated with blue, white, and yellow tiles as were many traditional Mexican kitchens. Beautiful clay pots and wooden spoons sat on the counters. On one wall, Kahlo hung many tiny clay cups so that they spelled out "Frida" and "Diego."

Inside and outside Casa Azul were large, brightly decorated Judas figures. According to the Bible, Judas was the disciple who betrayed Jesus. These figures are found everywhere in Mexico during Easter. On the Saturday before Easter Sunday (the day Christians celebrate Jesus' resurrection), ugly, colorful figures of Judas are hung up high after being filled or tied with firecrackers. Churches ring their bells at 10:00 A.M. on Holy Saturday, giving the signal to light the firecracker Judas.[4] The Judas figures can be seen in some of Kahlo's paintings.

Kahlo owned more than five hundred *retablos* or *ex-votos*, small paintings done on tin, thanking God or a saint for a miracle. Many Catholic churches in Mexico are filled with these paintings. Each retablo is about the size of a postcard. A retablo usually has three parts. At the top is the saint, the Virgin Mary, or God who brought about the miracle. In the center is a vivid drawing of the illness or disaster. Then at the bottom is a written description of what happened and a thank-you to the heavenly figure. Kahlo used some parts of this popular form of art in her own paintings. The painting which is most like a retablo is "Marxism Will Give Health to the Sick" (1954).

Kahlo also kept a beautiful garden full of colorful flowers and a large collection of animals. She had songbirds and parakeets, cats and dogs, monkeys, two turkeys, an eagle, and a deer as pets. One of her and Rivera's favorites was a spider monkey named Fulang Chang (meaning "any old monkey").[5] They allowed the pets inside the house and many of their friends remember sharing their meals with monkeys and parrots at the dining table. Another one of Kahlo's favorites, Bonito the parrot, made guests laugh by making his way through the clay pots and plates on the table to get to the butter, his favorite snack.

Every morning, Kahlo took time to choose what clothes and jewelry she was going to wear. She especially liked the clothes from Tehuantepec in Southern Mexico. These traditional dresses have bright colors, long flowing skirts, and are very festive. The Tehuana women are known for their personal strength, beauty, and independence. According to Mexican legend, Tehuana women are the ones who run the markets, take care of the money, and control the men.[6]

Kahlo had a very special style of dress. While she was in Paris in 1939, the fashion designer Elsa Schiaparelli saw her in her beautiful Mexican clothing

"Fulang-Chang and Me" (1937), oil on composition board

and created a dress in her name, *robe Madame Rivera*. Kahlo's style was even featured in *Vogue* magazine at the time.[7] Her hand, complete with rings, was on the front cover. However, many Mexican women and men did not like her style of dress. This was a time in Mexico when people dressed in very Western styles (modern clothes like those worn in the United States and Europe).[8] In 1948, a twenty-one-year-old bank worker said that "stylish people in Mexico think a rebozo [shawl] is the badge of a housemaid."[9] Still, Kahlo chose to wear her beautiful traditional Mexican clothing.

Because many of Kahlo's teeth were rotted and black, she often covered her mouth when she laughed. Some people feel that this is why she rarely smiled in photographs. For special occasions, Kahlo capped her teeth with gold and diamonds. One of her friends, Parker Lesley, remembers one evening at the Palace of Fine Arts:

> No one paid any attention to the dance performance . . . Everyone stared at Frida, who wore her Tehuana dress and all Diego's gold jewelry, and clanked like a knight in armor . . . She had two gold incisors [teeth] and when she was all gussied [dressed] up she would take off the plain gold caps and put on gold caps with rose diamonds in front, so that her smile really sparkled.[10]

Every morning, Kahlo took the time to comb, braid, and arrange her long, dark hair. Sometimes she wove

Frida Kahlo dressed as a Tehuana in front of part of her ceramics collection in Casa Azul's dining room.

brightly colored yarn through the braids. Other times she decorated her hair with flowers from her garden or with small combs she would buy at the market.

No outfit of Kahlo would be complete without a rebozo. Her rebozo was usually made out of silk or linen and Kahlo always chose a color that went well with the rest of her clothes. Her favorite rebozo was bright pink and handmade in Oaxaca,[11] a city in southern Mexico.

Friends and family remember the wonderful parties and meals that Kahlo prepared. Not only were the foods delicious, but Kahlo also made sure that the table was beautifully set with colorful Mexican dishes, glasses, and flowers. Because Kahlo celebrated so many different holidays, there was always an excuse to throw a party. One of Kahlo's favorite times of the year was Christmas. Each year at Christmas time, Kahlo arranged a *posada* (a party that is held in Mexico at Christmas).

In Mexico, the Christmas season starts on December 16. During the nine days leading up to December 24, the posadas re-enact the story of Mary and Joseph trying to find lodging. People take the roles of Mary and Joseph and walk from house to house singing "I am tired. I beg for rest." Those inside sing back "Go away, go away, there is no room."[12] After they are finally allowed in, a big fiesta takes place. Sweet drinks and delicious foods are served. Piñatas filled with candy and small toys are broken open. Kahlo's posadas were some of the best in Coyoacán.

To show her strong pride in her *mexicanidad*, Kahlo also celebrated many national or patriotic holidays. On March 21, Kahlo would celebrate Benito Juárez's birthday. Benito Juárez was a very popular president of Mexico from 1861 to 1872. He was the first native Mexican to hold such an important position. Juárez was known for his fight against the all-controlling power of the Catholic Church. He was especially admired for the many positive changes he brought to Mexico's poor.

September 16 is Independence Day in Mexico, marking Mexico's liberation from Spanish rule. At the beginning of the month, Kahlo would start buying small Mexican flags at the market. She would stick these little red, white, and green flags into fruits and plants all over the house as decorations. One of her favorite dishes during the national holiday was "national flag rice"—she would arrange white rice with rice colored red with tomatoes and rice stained green with chiles and herbs. She would serve this with colored drinks—green lime water, white rice water, and red Jamaica water (made with hibiscus flowers). Kahlo's guests were very delighted with her delicious patriotic food.[13]

Even though much of Kahlo's life was painful, she also enjoyed life very much. Despite her physical and emotional hardships, she found the beautiful and the joyous things that life offered.

"Viva La Vida"

Frida Kahlo often joked about death, calling it *la pelona* (the bald one). Many of her paintings feature skeletons and other symbols of death. These figures often appear in traditional Mexican art. Sometimes Kahlo showed how close death was to her by drawing it circling around her bed. She would buy candy skulls to celebrate the Day of the Dead (November 1) and have her and Rivera's names written across the forehead.

After her divorce and subsequent remarriage, Kahlo became sicker. In 1946, she traveled to New

York to have spinal surgery. Kahlo was put in a steel cast that she had to wear for eight months. Her doctors told her not to paint while she recuperated, but she did not listen to them and painted anyway.

Over the course of her lifetime, Kahlo had thirty-five operations.[1] She was made to wear twenty-eight corsets—one of them was made of steel, three of leather, and the rest of plaster.[2] To ease the pain, she had to take many different types of medicines. Toward the end of her life, Kahlo wrote in her diary, "I hope the exit is joyful—and I hope never to come back—Frida."[3]

On January 3, 1950, Kahlo woke up to find that four of the toes on her right foot had turned black on the ends. The pain in her back had also become unbearable. She checked into Mexico City's English Hospital after her doctors recommended another operation. She stayed in the hospital for a year recovering from the complicated surgery. During this time, Rivera stayed in a small room next to hers so he could be near her.

Kahlo passed the time in many ways. She decorated her room with the Soviet flag, flowers that were brought to her, and the candy sugar skulls that are traditionally sold in Mexico at the end of October. She had fun decorating her plaster corsets with feathers, mirrors, stickers, and, of course, paint. Kahlo had all her visitors sign the casts, too.

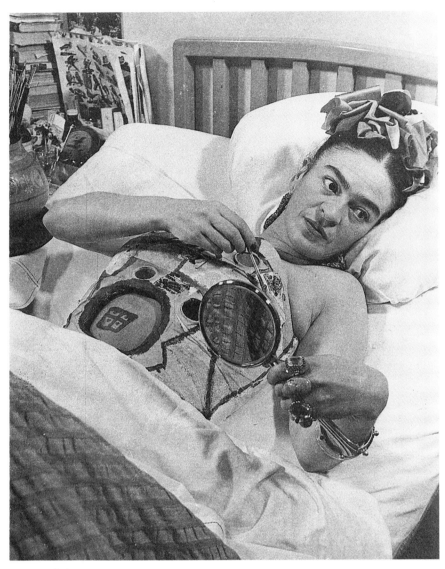

Kahlo decorating one of her plaster corsets while recuperating in the English Hospital, Mexico City, 1950. Photograph by Juan Guzmán.

Another way she kept herself entertained was by watching movies. Rivera borrowed a film projector and rented different films for Kahlo. Frida's sister, Cristina, brought huge lunch baskets filled with delicious Mexican food. Kahlo's friends and family remember how much fun they had in her hospital room eating, watching movies, and talking. Kahlo herself said: "I painted my plaster corsets and paintings, I joked around, I wrote, they brought me movies . . . it was a fiesta. I cannot complain."[4]

Toward the end of her year in the hospital, she said, "When I leave the hospital two months from now there are three things I want to do: paint, paint, paint."[5] When she finally left the hospital, she found that her failing energy and health did not allow her to paint for long. Using a cane or crutches, she could only walk for a little while and not very far. Mostly she moved around in her wheelchair, but even sitting became very painful after a while. A new wing was added to Casa Azul so that Kahlo could move between her bedroom and her studio without having to use the stairs.

As she grew older, her art changed in style and content. She became very passionate about socialist politics. In many of her still lifes, she included flags, political sayings, and other symbols. Also, because she was taking heavy pain medication, Kahlo's style became messier and lost the details characteristic of her earlier work. Some say that her art also suffered because she was in a hurry. In order to make money to buy her medicines or to help Rivera out financially, she needed to finish her paintings quickly in order to sell them.[6]

In the summer of 1953, doctors told Kahlo that gangrene had set in on her right leg. Gangrene is a disease that causes the flesh on certain parts of the body to die. They said that the leg would have to be cut off or else the disease could spread. After she was told that her right leg would have to be amputated, Kahlo courageously wrote in her diary: "Feet—what do I need them for if I have wings to fly?"[7] Rather than wait, Kahlo told the doctors to go ahead and remove the leg at once.

Since she was always active in political causes, Kahlo wanted to go to a political rally on July 2, 1954. When Kahlo's doctors heard about the rally, they told her she was too sick to leave her home, especially because it was cold outside. But Kahlo wanted to show her support along with the ten thousand other Mexicans at the rally. A photograph that was taken that night shows a very ill and old-looking Kahlo being pushed along in a wheelchair by Rivera. Because she had her leg amputated by then and was too weak to walk, she had to rely on the use of a wheelchair. After four hours in the chilly night air, Kahlo returned home very tired and became sicker.

Kahlo made her last public appearance at a political rally on July 2, 1954. To her right is Juan O'Gorman. Behind her with his hand on her shoulder is Diego Rivera.

Although Rivera was living with her at this time, Kahlo was also cared for by Cornelia Mayet, a nurse. Cornelia had to keep close watch on Kahlo because she would often take more medicine than the doctor prescribed. Cornelia remembers the last night she saw Kahlo alive:

> Frida usually put a bunch [of pills] in her mouth all at once. She was supposed to take only seven, so I told señor Diego that, and I counted the pills that were in the jar. As I left to sleep for a while in the [next] bedroom, the señora was giving him a ring she had hidden away as a present for him next August, when they would have celebrated their twenty-fifth wedding anniversary. The next day, I counted the pills. Eleven were gone. About six o'clock in the morning I heard the arrival of maestro Diego's assistant, Manuel. I left the bedroom and went toward Frida's bed. Her eyes were open, staring and looking toward one side. Her right arm was hanging out of bed. I touched her and cried out. She was cold. I shouted for Manuel to come upstairs. Then he went to the studio to tell señor Rivera what had happened.[8]

Kahlo was forty-seven years old when she died on July 13, 1954. The official cause of death was pulmonary embolism (when an air bubble blocks a blood vessel in the lungs). Still, some of Kahlo's friends feel she may have tried to kill herself.[9]

Rivera was crushed and locked himself in his

room, refusing to see anyone. He could not believe his "Chiquita" was dead. Afterward, he told his assistant on the San Francisco murals, Emmy Lou Packard, "I had no idea I was going to miss her so much."[10] Later, Rivera said, "Too late now I realized that the most wonderful part of my life had been my love for Frida."[11]

Kahlo's body was taken to the Palace of Fine Arts in Mexico City. There, under rainy skies, hundreds of mourners came to pay their last respects. Her body was eventually cremated. With her usual sense of humor, Kahlo had said that after all the corsets she had to wear while she was alive, she could not stand the thought of being stuffed into a coffin.[12]

Before being cremated, Kahlo's body was placed in a coffin for the funeral. Kahlo always said that she would want her coffin to be covered with the Mexican communist flag. When she died, friends and family made sure that the red flag with a gold hammer and sickle was draped over her coffin. Government officials were not happy about that, since they had warned Rivera not to make any mention of communist politics at the funeral. They threatened to remove it. In the end, Kahlo's wishes were respected and the flag stayed.

People who attended the funeral and cremation describe something very strange that happened. Kahlo's body was taken out of the coffin by Rivera

La Casa Azul in Coyoacán is now the Frida Kahlo Museum.

and placed on a cart that would be pushed into the cremation oven. As the body was slowly being rolled in, Kahlo's family and friends began to sing songs of farewell. Suddenly, when the powerful heat of the fire reached the body, the corpse sat bolt upright. People were amazed to see Kahlo's face framed by her blazing hair. Like her life, Kahlo's exit from this world was dramatic and unforgettable.

Today, Kahlo's ashes are kept in a very old vase, shaped like a headless woman, in Casa Azul, which is now the Frida Kahlo Museum. Kahlo's diary, paintings, and personal belongings are kept there, too. There is one closed room that contains many of Kahlo's and Rivera's private papers and letters and is off-limits to visitors.

"Viva La Vida" (1954) was one of the last pieces painted by Kahlo. It shows ripe red watermelons against a bright blue sky with the words "Long Live Life." This painting is still in Casa Azul today. It shows how even when she was close to death, Kahlo loved life and all the beautiful things in it.

"RIBBON AROUND A BOMB"

 In all, Kahlo made almost one hundred fifty paintings—many of them self-portraits. Although Kahlo painted most of the major events of her life, one exception was the streetcar accident in 1925. Although she did draw it, she never painted it. Kahlo felt that the accident was too complicated and important to make just one painting. The pencil drawing that she did shows that she must have been very upset because the lines are rough and uncontrolled.[1]

Kahlo did not plan on becoming a painter. As a child, she had set her sights on becoming a doctor. This interest in medicine and the human body can be seen in many of her paintings where she drew the human heart, veins, and other body parts and organs very exactly. For several of them, it is obvious that Kahlo looked at a medical book to paint such correct details. In fact, during her recovery at Henry Ford Hospital after her miscarriage, she asked her doctors for a medical book showing what an unborn fetus looked like. Her doctors refused, fearing that it would upset her. In the end, Rivera got the book for her and she used it to paint part of "Henry Ford Hospital" (1932).

Kahlo would take great care to draw very small details in her paintings. When she painted monkeys, she drew in each hair, one by one, and even included their fleas![2] When she drew plants, she made sure to paint every root, leaf, and stem. By using tiny brush strokes, taking her time, and carefully choosing colors, Kahlo created very detailed and precise paintings.

While she was alive, Kahlo had only two solo shows, that is, she was the only artist on exhibit. The first solo exhibition of Kahlo's paintings was in Manhattan, New York. It was held in November 1938, at the Julian Levy Gallery. The show was a great success and Kahlo was able to sell half of her paintings on exhibit.

Earlier that year, the French painter and poet André Breton and his wife, Jacqueline Lamba, visited Mexico. Breton was the leader of a group called the

Surrealists. The Surrealists painted art that seemed to come from their dreams and their subconscious (thoughts in our minds of which we are not aware). They did not try to control their thoughts but rather painted whatever came to their minds. When Breton met Kahlo and saw her work, he declared her to be a Surrealist because of the fantastic scenes depicted in her paintings. But in her later years, Kahlo said she was not. "I never painted dreams, I painted my own reality."[3]

In 1939, André Breton organized a special show in Paris of Mexican folk art, including some of Kahlo's paintings, called *Mexique.* Some people thought Kahlo's work was too shocking to be shown in public. Breton thought Kahlo's art was so powerful that he called it "a ribbon around a bomb."[4]

Kahlo did not enjoy her time in Paris.[5] At the opening of *Mexique,* Kahlo stayed mostly in the corner. Because she could not speak French, she could not talk with most of the people there. She was also dismayed that her seventeen paintings did not sell. Jacqueline Lamba Breton, André's wife, felt that this was in part due to the fact that at that time women painters were not highly valued—"It was very hard to be a woman painter."[6]

Not all of Kahlo's trip was a failure, however. During her trip to Paris she met Pablo Picasso, the famous Spanish painter. He gave her earrings in the shape of hands; she later painted two self-portraits in which she wore Picasso's gift. Also, the famous art museum, the Louvre, bought one of her paintings, "Self-Portrait: The Frame" (1938). Rivera boasted of his wife's achievement; no artist from Latin America, including himself, had been honored in such a way.

Despite her shows in New York and Paris, Kahlo had not had an exhibition in Mexico. The year before Kahlo died, her friend Lola Alvarez Bravo organized an art show to feature her paintings. When Kahlo found out about it she personally designed the invitations. The show was at the Galería de Arte Contemporáneo (Gallery of Contemporary Art), April 13–27, 1953.

Kahlo was very sick during this time. Her doctors told her to stay at home and not go to the show, but she would not hear of it. She sent her big, four-poster bed complete with decorations ahead of her to the show. Kahlo's thirty paintings and twenty drawings had to be rearranged to make room for it.

Hundreds of people went to the exhibition. A crowd of people lined up outside. Suddenly, the sirens of an ambulance and motorcycles were heard. Everyone was surprised to see Kahlo carried out of the ambulance and into the building on a stretcher. She was placed on her decorated bed, in her beautiful clothing and jewelry. Many friends and admirers walked past to greet her. To reporters from *Time* magazine she said: "I am not sick. I am broken. But I am happy to be alive as long as I can paint."[7] The reporter from *Time* said that the overall feeling of the show was that it was "a painful autobiography set down with brush and paint."[8]

As it got close to midnight, friends stood near her bed and sang Kahlo's favorite Mexican songs. Even though she was weak and was taking a lot of pain medicine, Kahlo reigned from her four-poster bed like a queen. The show was a big success and numerous art lovers within and outside of Mexico bought her paintings.

Because many of the events in Kahlo's life were sad or painful, many of her paintings were sad and painful, too. Also, although she and Rivera loved each other, he did not always treat her very well. Perhaps what might have made her the saddest of all was that she was not able to have children.[9] In all, Kahlo had three miscarriages.

Kahlo told a friend that when she and Rivera found out they could not have a child, she cried non-stop and busied herself by cooking, dusting, and accompanying Rivera while he painted.[10] Kahlo once said "I lost three children. . . . Paintings substituted for all of this. I believe that work is the best thing."[11] Some people believe that her best work was created out of this sadness over not being able to have children.[12]

Kahlo collected dolls that some say replaced the

baby she never had. She even kept a small empty bed next to her own where she once kept her favorite doll. One of Kahlo's paintings shows her sitting on a simple bed beside a naked doll ("Me and My Doll," 1937). Many times when her friends went on trips she would say "Remember to bring me a doll!" and they did.[13] Kahlo developed a very large collection of dolls from all over the world.

Kahlo's many pets also seemed to be a substitute for children. Many of her self-portraits feature her monkeys and parrots. In fact, Kahlo painted her self-portrait with monkeys at least eight times.[14] When Bonito, her parrot, died she wrote to her friend Emmy Lou Packard and told her of the burial she had given him and how much she had cried. She even included Bonito in one of her self-portraits ("Self-Portrait with Bonito," 1941).

Because she could not have children of her own, Kahlo took special delight in other people's children. She particularly spoiled Lupe and Ruth Rivera (Rivera's daughters with his previous wife, Lupe Marín) and Isolda and Antonio (her sister Cristina's children). Several of Kahlo's paintings feature children she knew.

After her divorce from Rivera in 1939, Kahlo became very sad and lonely. This sadness and loneliness, however, fueled some of her finest painting.[15] One of her most famous and largest paintings, "The

"The Two Fridas (Las Dos Fridas)" (1939), oil on canvas

Two Fridas (Las Dos Fridas)" (1939), was painted just a few months after her separation from Rivera.

Kahlo painted still lifes—fruits, vegetables, and flowers. She also painted portraits of friends and family and of people who commissioned her art. But the one thing Kahlo painted most was herself. Some people believe that she painted herself so much to make sure that she would be remembered. When asked why she painted so many self-portraits she answered, "because I am so often alone, because I am the subject I know best."[16]

It was difficult for Frida to understand why other people would be interested in her self-portraits. After all, she thought, the paintings were "by her, about her, and for her."[17] Who else would be interested in such personal work? She often called her paintings small and unimportant. The sculptor Isamu Noguchi, who was a friend of Kahlo, said that she was unsure about showing her paintings to others. Noguchi thought that Kahlo considered her paintings as a "private diary. I'm sure she never intended for them to be seen."[18]

During the 1930s and 1940s, most artists in Mexico were painting pieces that were very large and very public. Yet Kahlo decided to paint small, personal paintings on different kinds of surfaces such as metal, wood, glass, and cardboard, as well as canvas. "The Wounded Deer (The Little Deer)" (1946) is only 9 x 12 inches, yet it clearly shows the pain that Kahlo was feeling. In this painting, Kahlo is a deer that has been stabbed by many arrows. She is in a forest made up of trees that are cracked and dying. She sent "The Wounded Deer" to friends in New York along with a poem that included these lines:

> The deer walked alone
>
> very sad, and very wounded
>
> until in Arcady and Lina [Kahlo's friends]
>
> he found warmth and a nest.
>
> When the deer returns
>
> strong, happy and cured
>
> the wounds he has now
>
> will all be erased.[19]

Although Kahlo's style was very unusual, she was influenced by other painters. She admired the work of popular artists in Mexico such as José Guadalupe Posada, who was known for his funny prints of songs, poems, skeletons, and traditional Mexican designs. Posada also made prints of gruesome murders of the time and sold them for pennies to people who could not read or write.[20]

The influence of her large collection of retablos can also be seen in some of her work. The beauty of ancient Mexican art also found its way into Kahlo's art. She was also inspired by European painters such as Paul Gauguin, Salvador Dali, and Rene Magritte and the American painter Georgia O'Keeffe.

Kahlo's paintings were not well-known in the United States or England until the late 1970s. During that time, there was a growing awareness of women's issues. It is easy to see how art painted by such a strong woman, dealing with many women's problems, would catch the attention of lots of people. In 1976, her image was used to represent the "International Year of the Woman."[21] She continues to be a hero for many Hispanics and women of all cultures.

In 1978, the Museum of Contemporary Art in Chicago had a show of Kahlo's work. This show was organized by Hayden Herrera, an author who later published the most complete biography of Kahlo to date. Many Americans learned of Kahlo's work for the first time. Many of them soon fell in love with her art.

Then, in 1982, an art gallery in London put on another exhibition of Kahlo's work. This show also included photographs by Tina Modotti, Kahlo's friend in the Communist party. This European exhibition was the first show to feature Kahlo's work since Mexique in Paris in 1939. Additionally, shows were held in Germany, Japan, and France. Now there are lovers of Kahlo's art all over the world.

Although it may seem that Kahlo's art is just becoming popular in the United States, many Americans have always appreciated her work. The actor and art collector Edward G. Robinson bought four of her paintings in 1938 for two hundred dollars each.[22]

Interestingly, most of Kahlo's art collectors are women.[23] Today, the pop singer Madonna is one of the greatest collectors of Kahlo's art—she has paid about one million dollars for "My Birth" (1932). It is said that Madonna has asked for a screenplay for a movie based on Kahlo's life in which she plans to star.[24] Madonna even visited Alejandro Gómez Arias before his death in 1990 and asked him to share his "secrets about Frida." The pop singer was also quoted as saying that "She [Kahlo] is my obsession and my inspiration."[25]

Kahlo's art has become so popular that in 1990 Kahlo's painting, "Diego and I," sold for a record-breaking $1.43 million. It was the first piece of art from Latin America to break the million-dollar mark. In 1991, Kahlo's "Self-Portrait with Loose Hair" sold for $1.65 million; the proceeds of that sale were donated to start a women's studies center at the University of Iowa.[26] Since then, one of her self-portraits has sold for over $3 million and her 170-page personal diary has sold for over $100,000.[27]

The diary that she kept from 1944 until her death is especially interesting because it is filled with illustrations and poems by Kahlo as well as her writing. For many years, no one was allowed to read it, and it was locked in a glass box for visitors in Casa Azul. After several years, a young Mexican artist named Claudia Madrazo finally persuaded Dolores Olmedo, the executor of Kahlo's and Rivera's estate, to authorize the diary's publication.[28] Frida Kahlo lovers now have a rare opportunity to explore her life from Kahlo's own point of view.

The value of Kahlo's work has prompted the Mexican government to declare it "national patrimony." This means that her art can only be loaned for exhibition abroad—it cannot leave Mexico permanently.

There have been several plays and films produced on Kahlo's life and art. One play, written by Claire Braz-Valentine, is called *When Will I Dance*. It is based on Kahlo's memory of her childhood imaginary friend, a healthy girl the same age as Kahlo who could dance. Because of this, the play has only two characters—Kahlo and her imaginary friend. A 1983 film, *Frida Kahlo: Portrait of an Artist*, recounts Kahlo's life and gives an analysis of her work. *Frida Kahlo: A Ribbon Around a Bomb* is a 1992 film that blends interviews, photographs, and Kahlo's paintings. To date, there have been at least eighty-seven books written on Kahlo's life and art.

Popular fashion magazines have published stories on the influence of Kahlo's style of dress on modern clothing. For example, *Elle* magazine (May 1989) printed an article on modern clothes inspired by Kahlo's fashion. The February 1990 issue of *Vogue* similarly tried to capture the "romance" of Kahlo's style.

Angélica Díaz of Angelica's Mexican Cafe poses in front of a painting she created featuring Frida Kahlo.

There is even a restaurant in West Hollywood, California, called "Little Frida's" where you can order dishes inspired by the artist, like a "Frida Salad." The style of the restaurant reminds one of the blue walls and folk art of Casa Azul.[29] In Miami, Florida, there is a Mexican restaurant that has one night of the week dedicated to "Frida's Fiestas." On this night, they serve dishes that Kahlo used to make and enjoy. Angelica's Cafe in Tampa, Florida, pays tribute to Kahlo by hosting a look-alike contest, poetry reading, and cooking some of Kahlo's favorite recipes on the anniversaries of her birth and death. The restaurant owner, Angélica Díaz, even created a painting that features Kahlo.[30]

When her friend Lucienne Bloch was asked what Kahlo would think about the United States' "Frida mania" she said, "She would have a big laugh. Kahlo would say, 'Look at those crazy gringos!'"[31]

Although Kahlo died in 1954, we have her art to remember her by. It is not always pretty and it is sometimes painful and frightening, but it is also a reminder of strength and courage. At Kahlo's funeral, Andrés Iduarte, the director of the National Institute of Fine Arts and a former Cachucha, ended his memorial speech this way: "Friend, sister of the people, great daughter of Mexico: you are still alive."[32]

CHRONOLOGY

1907—Frida is born on July 6 to Matilde Calderón y González and Guillermo Kahlo in Coyoacán, Mexico.

1910—The Mexican Revolution erupts. Later on, Frida begins telling people that she was born in 1910, taking three years off her age.

1913—Doctors say Frida has polio, which affects her right leg.

1922—Frida attends the National Preparatory School, "La Prepa." At La Prepa, she joins the student group "Los Cachuchas." During her time there, she watches the great muralist painter Diego Rivera work in the school auditorium.

1925—On September 17, Frida is in a horrible bus accident that changes her life forever.

1926—While she is recovering from the accident, Frida begins to paint. **Major Work:** "Self-Portrait Wearing a Velvet Dress."

1928—Kahlo visits Diego Rivera to get his opinion of her painting. He tells her she has talent and should continue. **Major Works:** "Portrait of Cristina Kahlo," "Two Women."

1929—Kahlo and Rivera marry on August 21; Rivera is forty years old and Kahlo is twenty-two. **Major Works:** "The Bus," "Portrait of a Girl."

1930—The couple travel to the United States. Rivera works on murals in San Francisco. **Major Work:** "Self-Portrait."

1931— Kahlo meets Dr. Leo Eloesser, who becomes her life-long friend and medical advisor. Kahlo's work is included in a group show at the Sixth Annual Exhibition of the San Francisco Society of Women Artists. In November, Kahlo and Rivera go to New York for Rivera's exhibition at the Museum of Modern Art. **Major Works:** "Portrait of Mrs. Jean Wight," "Frida and Diego," "Portrait of Luther Burbank."

1932— Kahlo travels with Rivera to Detroit. Rivera paints murals at the Detroit Institute of Arts. While in Detroit, Kahlo is hospitalized due to a miscarriage. Kahlo's mother dies. **Major Works:** "Henry Ford Hospital," "Self-Portrait on the Border Between Mexico and the United States," "My Birth."

1933— Kahlo and Rivera move to New York where Rivera begins work at the Rockefeller Center. **Major Works:** "Self-Portrait with Necklace," "My Dress Hangs There."

1934—Kahlo has the first operation on her right foot since the bus accident in 1925. Kahlo and Rivera move into the twin houses in San Angel when they return from the United States. When she finds out about Diego and Cristina's love affair, she becomes very depressed and does not paint anything during this year.

1935— Kahlo has second operation on right foot. Frida and Diego separate after Diego's affair with Cristina. **Major Work:** "A Few Small Nips."

1936— Kahlo has a third operation on her right foot. **Major Work:** "My Grandparents, My Parents, and I (Family Tree)."

1937— Leon Trotsky arrives in Mexico. Kahlo meets him and his wife, Natalia Sedova, in Tampico Harbor and brings them back to Casa Azul. **Major Works:** "Portrait of Diego Rivera," "Me and My Doll," "Fulang Chang and Me," "Self-Portrait Dedicated to Leon Trotsky," "The Deceased Dimas," "Memory," "My Nanny and I."

1938— Kahlo travels to New York where she has her first solo art exhibition at the Levy Gallery. **Major Works:** "Tunas," "Self-Portrait: The Frame," "Self-Portrait with Monkey," "The Suicide of Dorothy Hale," "What the Water Gave Me."

1939— Kahlo participates in the art show *Mexique* in Paris. The Louvre buys her painting "Self-Portrait: The Frame." Kahlo and Rivera officially divorce in November. Rivera and Trotsky argue and Trotsky moves out of Casa Azul. When Kahlo returns from Paris she moves into Casa Azul. **Major Work:** "Las Dos Fridas."

1940— Trotsky is assassinated. While in San Francisco, Kahlo and Rivera remarry. **Major Works:** "Self-Portrait with Cropped Hair," "Self-Portrait with Thorn Necklace," "Self-Portrait with Monkey," "Self-Portrait Dedicated to Sigmund Firestone," "Self-Portrait Dedicated to Doctor Eloesser," "The Dream."

1941— Kahlo's father dies. Kahlo and Rivera move into Casa Azul. **Major Works:** "Self-Portrait with Bonito," "Self-Portrait with Braid," "Self-Portrait."

1943—Kahlo begins working as a teacher at La Esmeralda. Los Fridos paint the pulquería La Rosita. **Major Works:** "Self-Portrait with Monkeys," "Diego in My Thoughts," "The Bride Frightened at Seeing Life Opened," "Thinking of Death," "Roots."

1944—Kahlo begins keeping a diary. **Major Works:** "Six Portraits of the Morillo Safa family," "The Broken Column," "Diego and Frida 1929–1944."

1945—Los Fridos begin painting murals at a public laundry house in Coyoacán. **Major Works:** "Moses," "Self-Portrait with Small Monkey," "The Mask," "Without Hope," "Magnolias," "The Chick."

1946—Kahlo goes to New York for spinal surgery and has to wear a steel cast for eight months. She is one of six artists awarded the Mexican National Prize of Arts and Sciences. **Major Works:** "The Wounded Deer," "Tree of Hope Stand Firm."

1947—Kahlo's "Diego in My Thoughts" is included in an exhibition featuring self-portraits by Mexican painters at the National Institute of Fine Arts. **Major Work:** "Self-Portrait with Unbound Hair."

1949—**Major Work:** "Diego and I."

1950—Kahlo spends most of the year in the hospital because of spinal surgery and infections.

1953—The only solo exhibition in Mexico of Kahlo's work is held in Mexico's Galería de Arte Contemporáneo. Due to gangrene, Kahlo's right leg is amputated. **Major Works:** "Fruit of Life," "Still Life with Watermelons."

1954— Kahlo goes to a rally to protest the United States' role in Guatemala. Eleven days later, on July 13th, she dies in Coyoacán at the age of forty-seven. **Major Works:** "Viva La Vida," "Self-Portrait with Stalin," "Marxism Will Give Health to the Sick," "The Brick Ovens."

CHAPTER NOTES

CHAPTER 1

1. Martha Zamora, *Frida Kahlo: The Brush of Anguish* (San Francisco: Chronicle Books, 1990), p. 23.

2. Hayden Herrera, *Frida: A Biography of Frida Kahlo* (New York: Harper and Row Publishers, 1983), p. 48.

3. Ibid., p. 49.

4. Bertram D. Wolfe, *The Fabulous Life of Diego Rivera* (New York: Stein and Day, 1963), p. 242.

5. Elena Paniatowska and Carla Stellweg, *Frida Kahlo: The Camera Seduced* (San Francisco: Chronicle Books, 1992), p. 17.

6. Erika Billeter quoting Raquel Tibol, *The Blue House: The World of Frida Kahlo* (Frankfurt, Germany: Schirn Kunsthalle, 1993), p. 245.

CHAPTER 2

1. Frida's name was originally spelled "Frieda," the traditional German spelling. Later, when the Nazis rose to power, she dropped the "e" to make the name look less German.

2. Raquel Tibol, *Frida Kahlo: Una Vida Abierta* (Mexico: Editorial Oasis, 1983), p. 32.

3. Guillermo Kahlo's original name was Wilhelm Kahlo. He changed it soon after he arrived in Mexico so that it sounded more Spanish.

4. Elena Paniatowska and Carla Stellweg, *Frida Kahlo: The Camera Seduced* (San Francisco: Chronicle Books, 1992), p. 106.

5. Hayden Herrera, *Frida Kahlo: The Paintings* (New York: HarperCollins Publishers, 1991), p. 18.

6. Leslie Sills, *Inspirations: Stories About Women Artists* (Niles, Ill.: Albert Whitman and Company, 1989), p. 18.

7. Herrera, p. 29.

8. Carla Stellweg, "The Camera's Seductress," in Paniatowska and Stellweg, p. 107.

9. Ibid., p. 106.

10. Herrera, p. 23.

11. Paniatowska and Stellweg, p. 17.

CHAPTER 3

1. Hayden Herrera, *Frida: A Biography of Frida Kahlo* (New York: Harper and Row Publishers, 1983), p. 25.

2. Martha Zamora, *Frida Kahlo: The Brush of Anguish* (San Francisco: Chronicle Books, 1990), p. 20.

3. Alejandro Gómez Arias, *Frida Kahlo and Tina Modotti* (London: Whitechapel Art Gallery, 1982), p. 38.

4. Zamora, p. 22.

5. Ibid.

6. Bertram D. Wolfe, *The Fabulous Life of Diego Rivera* (New York: Stein and Day, 1963), p. 241.

7. Zamora, p. 22.

8. Ibid.

9. Ibid.

10. Herrera, p. 31.

11. Zamora, p. 23.

12. Ibid., p. 22.

13. Ibid., p. 30.

14. Herrera, pp. 60–61.

CHAPTER 4

1. Martha Zamora, *Frida Kahlo: The Brush of Anguish* (San Francisco: Chronicle Books, 1990), p. 37.

2. Diego Rivera, *My Art, My Life: An Autobiography* (New York: The Citadel Press, 1960), p. 169.

3. Zamora, pp. 31, 34.

4. Ibid., p. 34.

5. Bertram D. Wolfe, *The Fabulous Life of Diego Rivera* (New York: Stein and Day, 1963), p. 247.

6. Zamora, p. 37.

7. Hayden Herrera, *Frida: A Biography of Frida Kahlo* (New York: Harper and Row Publishers, 1983), p. 98.

8. Ibid., pp. 98–99.

9. Zamora, p. 38.

10. Guadalupe Rivera and Marie-Pierre Colle, *Frida's Fiestas: Recipes and Reminiscences of Life with Frida Kahlo* (New York: Clarkson Potter Publishers, 1994), p. 12.

11. Ibid., p. 32.

12. Elena Paniatowska and Carla Stellweg, *Frida Kahlo: The Camera Seduced* (San Francisco: Chronicle Books, 1992), p. 111.

13. "Fashion Notes," *Time*, May 3, 1948, pp. 33–34.

14. Herrera, p. 361.

15. Ibid., pp. 402–403.

16. Malka Drucker, *Frida Kahlo: Torment and Triumph in Her Life and Art* (New York: Bantam Books, 1991), p. 92.

17. Erika Billeter, ed., *The Blue House: The World of Frida Kahlo* (Frankfurt, Germany: Schirn Kunsthalle, 1993), p. 250.

18. Drucker, p. 85.

19. Zamora, p. 50.

20. Herrera, p. 274.

21. Zamora, p. 70.

22. Leslie Sills, *Inspirations: Stories About Women Artists* (Niles, Ill.: Albert Whitman and Company, 1989), p. 24.

23. Herrera, p. 301.

24. Zamora, p. 70.

25. Ibid., p. 86.

26. Wolfe, p. 358.

27. Rivera, p. 287.

CHAPTER 5

1. Edward Weston, as quoted by Carla Stellweg, "The Camera's Seductress," in Paniatowska and Stellweg, *Frida Kahlo: The Camera Seduced* (San Francisco: Chronicle Books, 1992), p. 111.

2. Hayden Herrera, *Frida: A Biography of Frida Kahlo* (New York: Harper and Row Publishers, 1983), p. 234.

3. Ibid., p. 120.

4. Ibid., p. 118.

5. Diego Rivera, *My Art, My Life: An Autobiography* (New York: The Citadel Press, 1960), p. 241.

6. Herrera, p. 134.

7. Ibid., p. 135.

8. Herrera, p. 136.

9. Malka Drucker, *Frida Kahlo: Torment and Triumph in Her Life and Art* (New York: Bantam Books, 1991), p. 54.

10. Herrera, pp. 130–131.

11. Ibid., p. 155.

12. Rivera, p. 209.

13. Joseph Lilly, "Rivera Paints Scenes of Communist Activity and John D. Jr. Foots Bill," *New York World-Telegram*, April 24, 1933.

14. Herrera, p. 192.

CHAPTER 6

1. Rupert García, *Frida Kahlo: A Bibliography* (Berkeley, Calif.: Chicano Studies Library Publications Unit, 1983), p. 14.

2. Alejandro Gómez Arias, *Frida Kahlo and Tina Modotti* (London: Whitechapel Art Gallery, 1982), p. 27.

3. Martha Zamora, *Frida Kahlo: The Brush of Anguish* (San Francisco: Chronicle Books, 1990), p. 31.

4. Barbara Rose, "Frida Kahlo: The Chicana as Art Heroine," *Vogue*, April 1983, p. 152.

5. Zamora, p. 93.

6. Ibid., p. 42.

7. Bertram D. Wolfe, *The Fabulous Life of Diego Rivera* (New York: Stein and Day, 1963), p. 238.

8. Hayden Herrera, *Frida Kahlo: The Paintings* (New York: HarperCollins Publishers, 1991), p. 58.

9. Hayden Herrera, *Frida: A Biography of Frida Kahlo* (New York: Harper and Row Publishers, 1983), p. 330.

10. Ibid., p. 342.

11. Ibid., p. 343.

12. Malka Drucker, *Frida Kahlo: Torment and Triumph in Her Life and Art* (New York: Bantam Books, 1991), p. 91.

13. Herrera, *Frida: A Biography of Frida Kahlo*, p. 394.

14. Ibid., p. 425.

15. Ibid., p. 430.

16. Ibid., p. 342.

CHAPTER 7

1. Martha Zamora, *Frida Kahlo: The Brush of Anguish* (San Francisco: Chronicle Books, 1990), p. 8.

2. Ibid., p. 86.

3. Hayden Herrera, *Frida: A Biography of Frida Kahlo* (New York: Harper and Row Publishers, 1983), p. 162.

4. Elizabeth Silverthorne, *Fiesta!: Mexico's Great Celebrations* (Brookfield, Conn.: Millbrook Press, 1992), pp. 29–30.

5. Herrera, p. 196.

6. Ibid., p. 109.

7. Bertram D. Wolfe, "Rise of Another Rivera," *Vogue*, November 1, 1938, pp. 64, 131.

8. Jorge Alberto Lozoya, "Frida Kahlo and Ambiguity," in Erika Billeter, ed., *The Blue House: The World of Frida Kahlo* (Frankfurt, Germany: Schirn Kunsthalle, 1993), p. 71.

9. "Fashion Notes," *Time*, May 3, 1948, p. 34.

10. Herrera, p. 275.

11. Guadalupe Rivera and Marie-Pierre Colle, *Frida's Fiestas: Recipes and Reminiscences of Life with Frida Kahlo* (New York: Clarkson Potter Publishers, 1994), p. 30.

12. Silverthorne, p. 23.

13. Rivera and Colle, p. 49.

CHAPTER 8

1. Hayden Herrera, "Why Frida Kahlo Speaks to the 90's," *The New York Times*, October 28, 1990, Section 2, p. 41.

2. Hayden Herrera, *Frida: A Biography of Frida Kahlo* (New York: Harper and Row Publishers, 1983), pp. 345–346.

3. Malka Drucker, *Frida Kahlo: Torment and Triumph in Her Life and Art* (New York: Bantam Books, 1991), p. 143.

4. Herrera, *Frida: A Biography of Frida Kahlo*, p. 391.

5. Ibid., p. 389.

6. Ibid., p. 399.

7. Ibid., p. 414.

8. Martha Zamora, *Frida Kahlo: The Brush of Anguish* (San Francisco: Chronicle Books, 1990), p. 12.

9. Hayden Herrera, *Frida Kahlo: The Paintings* (New York: HarperCollins Publishers, 1991), p. 219.

10. Zamora, p. 13.

11. Diego Rivera, *My Art, My Life: An Autobiography* (New York: The Citadel Press, 1960), p. 287.

12. Hedda Garza, *Hispanics of Achievement: Frida Kahlo* (New York: Chelsea House, 1994), p. 112.

CHAPTER 9

1. Hayden Herrera, *Frida: A Biography of Frida Kahlo* (New York: Harper and Row Publishers, 1983), p. 74.

2. Elena Paniatowska and Carla Stellweg, *Frida Kahlo: The Camera Seduced* (San Francisco: Chronicle Books, 1992), p. 20.

3. Martha Zamora, *Frida Kahlo: The Brush of Anguish* (San Francisco: Chronicle Books, 1990), p. 114.

4. André Breton, as quoted by Hayden Herrera in *Frida: A Biography of Frida Kahlo*, p. 214.

5. Herrera, pp. 250–252.

6. Ibid., p. 250.

7. Zamora, p. 126.

8. "Art," *Time*, April 27, 1953, p. 90.

9. Leslie Sills, *Inspirations: Stories About Women Artists* (Niles, Ill.: Albert Whitman and Company, 1989), p. 24.

10. Herrera, p. 106.

11. Ibid., p. 148.

12. Edward J. Sullivan, "Frida Kahlo in New York," *Arts Magazine*, vol. 57, no. 7, March 1983, p. 92.

13. Herrera, p. 147.

14. Nancy Breslow, "Frida Kahlo: A Cry of Joy and Pain," *Americas*, vol. 32, March 1980, p. 38.

15. Zamora, p. 64.

16. Herrera, p. 74.

17. Malka Drucker, *Frida Kahlo: Torment and Triumph in Her Life and Art* (New York: Bantam Books, 1991), p. 72.

18. Ibid., p. 89.

19. Hayden Herrera, *Frida Kahlo: The Paintings* (New York: HarperCollins Publishers, 1991), p. 188.

20. Sarah M. Lowe, *Frida Kahlo* (New York: Universe Publishing, 1991), p. 83.

21. Mabel Montoya Barragan, "De Donde surgió la leyenda, restauran casa de Frida Kahlo," *El Nuevo Herald*, July 4, 1995, p. 4C.

22. Judd Tully, "The Kahlo Cult," *Art News*, April, 1994, p. 128.

23. Ibid., p. 133.

24. Janis Bergman-Carton, "Like an Artist," *Art in America*, vol. 81, January 1993, pp. 35–37.

25. Peter Plagens, Barbara Belejack, and John Taliaferro, "Frida on Our Minds" *Newsweek*, May 27, 1991, p. 54.

26. "Frida Fever," *Southwest Art*, vol. 21, August 1991, p. 23.

27. Jason Edward Kaufman, "Six-Figure Sum for Frida Kahlo's Journal," *The Art Newspaper*, vol. 42, November 1994, p. 23.

28. Juan Carlos Pérez, "El Ultimo Compañero de Frida," *El Nuevo Herald,* October 4, 1995, p. 2D.

29. Tully, p. 126.

30. Cloe Cabrera, "Cafe plans tribute to Mexican Artist," *The Tampa Tribune*, July 11, 1995, University section, p. 8.

31. Tully, p. 133.

32. Hedda Garza, *Hispanics of Achievement: Frida Kahlo* (New York: Chelsea House, 1994), p. 113.

FURTHER READING

Cockcroft, James D. *Hispanics of Achievement: Diego Rivera*. New York: Chelsea House, 1991.

Drucker, Malka. *Frida Kahlo: Torment and Triumph in Her Life and Art*. New York: Bantam, 1991.

Frazier, Nancy. *Frida Kahlo: Mysterious Painter*. (Woodbridge, Conn.: Blackbirch Press, 1992.

Garza, Hedda. *Hispanics of Achievement: Frida Kahlo*. New York: Chelsea House, 1994.

Gonzales, Doreen. *Diego Rivera: His Art, His Life*. Springfield, N.J.: Enslow Publishers, 1996.

Hargrove, Jim. *Diego Rivera*. Chicago: Children's Press, 1990.

Herrera, Hayden. *Frida: A Biography of Frida Kahlo*. New York: Harper and Row Publishers, 1983.

Jones, Jane Anderson. *The Arts: Frida Kahlo*. Vero Beach, Fla.: Rourke, 1993.

Sills, Leslie. *Inspirations: Stories About Women Artists*. Niles, Ill.: Albert Whitman and Company, 1989.

Turner, Robyn Montana. *Portraits of Women Artists for Children: Frida Kahlo*. Boston: Little, Brown, and Company, 1993.

Wolfe, Bertram D. *The Fabulous Life of Diego Rivera*. New York: Stein and Day, 1963.

BIBLIOGRAPHY

Arias, Alejandro Gómez. *Frida Kahlo and Tina Modotti*. London: Whitechapel Art Gallery, 1982.

"Art." *Time* (April 27, 1953), 9

Baddeley, Oriana. "Frida Kahlo." *The Oxford Art Journal*. vol. 14, no. 1, January 1991, 10–17.

Barragan, Mabel Montoya. "De Donde surgió la leyenda, restauran casa de Frida Kahlo." *El Nuevo Herald* (July 4, 1995), 4C.

Bergman-Carton, Janis. "Like an Artist." *Art in America*. vol. 81 (January 1993), 35–37.

Billeter, Erika, ed. *The Blue House: The World of Frida Kahlo*. Frankfurt, Germany: Schirn Kunsthalle, 1993.

"Bomb Beribboned." *Time* (November 19, 1938), 29.

Breslow, Nancy. "Frida Kahlo: A Cry of Joy and Pain." *Americas*. vol. 32 (March 1980), 33–39.

Cabrera, Cloe. "Cafe plans tribute to Mexican Artist." *The Tampa Tribune* (July 11, 1995), University section, 8.

Chadwick, Whitney. *Women Artists and the Surrealist Movement*. Boston: Little, Boston, and Company, 1985.

Drucker, Malka. *Frida Kahlo: Torment and Triumph in Her Life and Art*. New York: Bantam Books, 1991.

"Fashion Notes." *Time* (May 3, 1948), 33–34.

"Free La Frida." *Southwest Art*, vol. 21 (March 1992), 18, 20.

"Frida Fever." *Southwest Art,* vol. 21 (August 1991), 23.

"Frida vs. Diego." *Art Digest*, vol. 14 (November 1, 1939), 8.

García, Rupert. *Frida Kahlo: A Bibliography*. Berkeley: Chicano Studies Library Publications Unit, 1983.

Garza, Hedda. *Hispanics of Achievement: Frida Kahlo.* New York: Chelsea House, 1994.

Grimberg, Salomon. "Frida Kahlo's Memory." *Women's Art Journal* (Fall 1990/Winter 1991), 3–7.

Hargrove, Jim. *Diego Rivera.* Chicago: Children's Press, 1990.

Herrera, Hayden. *Frida: A Biography of Frida Kahlo*. New York: Harper and Row Publishers, 1983.

———. *Frida Kahlo: The Paintings*. New York: Harper Collins Publishers, 1991.

———. "Why Frida Kahlo Speaks to the 90's." *The New York Times* (October 28, 1990), Section 2, 1, 41.

Jenkins, Nicholas. "Calla Lilies and Kahlos." *Art News*, vol. 90 (March 1991), 104–105.

Kaufman, Jason Edward. "Six-Figure Sum for Frida Kahlo's Journal." *The Art Newspaper (42)* (November 1994).

Kozloff, Joyce. "Frida Kahlo." *Women's Studies*, vol. 6 (1978), 43–59.

Lilly, Joseph. "Rivera Paints Scenes of Communist Activity and John D. Jr. Foots Bill." *New York World-Telegram* (April 24, 1933).

Lowe, Sarah M. *Frida Kahlo*. New York: Universe Publishing, 1991.

Lozoya, Jorge Alberto. "Frida Kahlo and Ambiguity," in Erika Billeter, ed., *The Blue House: The World of Frida Kahlo*. Frankfurt, Germany: Schirn Kunsthalle, 1993, 71–72.

MacAdam, Barbara. "Before Diego." *Art News*, vol. 90 (Summer 1994), 30.

Monsiváis, Carlos, and Rafael Vázquez Bayod. *Frida Kahlo: Una Vida, Una Obra*. Mexico: Consejo Nacional Para La Cultura y Las Artes, 1992.

Paniatowska, Elena, and Carla Stellweg. *Frida Kahlo: The Camera Seduced*. San Francisco: Chronicle Books, 1992.

Pérez, Juan Carlos. "El Ultimo Compañero de Frida." *El Nuevo Herald* (October 4, 1995), Section D, 1D, 2D.

Plagens, Peter, Barbara Belejack, and John Taliaferro. "Frida on Our Minds." *Newsweek* (May 27, 1991), 54–55.

Rivera, Diego (with Gladys March). *My Art, My Life: An Autobiography*. New York: The Citadel Press, 1960.

Rivera, Guadalupe, and Marie-Pierre Colle. *Frida's Fiestas: Recipes and Reminiscences of Life with Frida Kahlo*. New York: Clarkson Potter Publishers, 1994.

Rose, Barbara. "Frida Kahlo: The Chicana as Art Heroine." *Vogue* (April 1983), 152–154.

Shapiro, William E., ed. *Lenin and Trotsky*. New York: Franklin Watts, Inc., 1967.

Sills, Leslie. *Inspirations: Stories About Women Artists.* Niles, Ill.: Albert Whitman & Company, 1989.

Silverthorne, Elizabeth. *Fiesta!: Mexico's Great Celebrations.* Brookfield, Conn: Millbrook Press, 1992.

Sullivan, Edward J. "Frida Kahlo in New York." *Arts Magazine,* vol. 57, no. 7 (March 1983), 90–92.

Tibol, Raquel. *Frida Kahlo: Una Vida Abierta.* Mexico: Editorial Oasis, 1983.

Tully, Judd. "The Kahlo Cult." *Art News* (April 1994), 126–133.

Turner, Robyn Montana. *Portraits of Women Artists for Children: Frida Kahlo.* Boston: Little, Brown, and Company, 1993.

Wolfe, Bertram D. *The Fabulous Life of Diego Rivera.* New York: Stein and Day, 1963.

Wolfe, Bertram D. "Rise of Another Rivera." *Vogue* (November 1, 1938), 64, 131.

Zamora, Martha. *Frida Kahlo: The Brush of Anguish.* San Francisco: Chronicle Books, 1990.

Zehme, Bill. "Madonna: White Heat." *Rolling Stone* (March 23, 1989), 50–58, 180–182.

INDEX